ESL ESOL EFL ELL

English Language Learning

with

A WORKBOOK

For ESL / ESOL / EFL / ELL Students

Beginners – Book 2

CHRIS BALLI

All illustrations are by Chris Balli and are copyright © 2017 by Griselda Califa.

ISBN: 978-0-692-99645-4

1. English Language - Beginner's text for foreign speakers   2. Beginning ESL / ESOL / EFL / ELL Student's Workbook 3. English Language - Basic Exercises and Activities 4. Beginning Literacy

Acknowledgements: My profound gratitude to these people for their assistance, encouragement, and continued support: G. Balli, I. Balli, I. Balli, S. Balli, K. Califa, and M. Califa.

And a special thank you to J. Castro for editing and professional suggestions, and to K. Wynne for editing, professional suggestions, and classroom feedback.

Table of Contents

Table of Contents

Table of Contents

Table of Contents

Chapter #6: Simple Present Tense - Questions

An Introduction for Teachers

Objective:

The primary objective of this book is communication, which includes speaking, reading, and writing. The language structures found in this workbook were specifically designed for immediate use in authentic, everyday situations. This book provides the necessary language needed for these everyday situations. As in life, skills such as driving or typing or learning a new language are acquired through constant practice and repetition. The lessons in this book were constructed with this in mind: that repetition and practice, in many varied drills and exercises, will maximize student learning.

Content:

The lessons, activities, and worksheets build on each other and get more difficult in tiny, incremental steps. The beginning lessons deal with personal information that every student should know and be able to communicate. Consequently, this was the perfect material for use in class surveys, pair-reporting, and drills. Right from the start, students get a sample of the activities and written lessons that will be used throughout the book. They also get an opportunity to practice speaking immediately. They will be practicing something that is relevant and necessary and more than a random language drill.

Target Audience:

This book is for basic and beginning ESL students. It is for zero-English speakers or minimal-English speakers. ESL students with complete educations from their own countries do not always require the entire set of exercises provided. Lessons can be selected to target specific trouble spots or for additional practice and reinforcement. ESL students from war-torn countries, illiterate students, or students with gaps in their educations will benefit from doing the entire set of exercises in this book. This material has been very effective in helping all of these groups.

What You Can Expect:

You can expect students to start speaking sooner than usual. You can expect vocabulary development for an improvement in reading. You can also expect students to advance quickly in writing independently. This book works!

Chapter #1

Sports and Recreation

Overview of Chapter #1
Review of the Present Continuous

1. Affirmative Sentences: To make an affirmative sentence, use a subject, a **"to be"** verb (**"am,"** **"are,"** or **"is"**), and the **"ing"** form of a verb. Examples:

Subject	+	am / are / is	+	"ing" form of a verb
I		am		swimming.
You		are		swimming.
He		is		swimming.
She		is		swimming.
It		is		swimming.
We		are		swimming.
You		are		swimming.
They		are		swimming.

2. Questions: To make a question, move the **"to be"** verb to the beginning of the sentence. Examples:

Am / Are / Is	+	Subject	+	"ing" form of a verb
Am		I		swimming?
Are		you		swimming?
Is		he		swimming?
Is		she		swimming?
Is		it		swimming?
Are		we		swimming?
Are		you		swimming?
Are		they		swimming?

3. Sports and Recreation Vocabulary

basketball	fishing	skiing	tennis
baseball	football	soccer	video games
bowling	(the) guitar	swimming	volleyball
cards	skateboarding	riding a bike	
checkers	skating	running / jogging	

Sports and Recreation

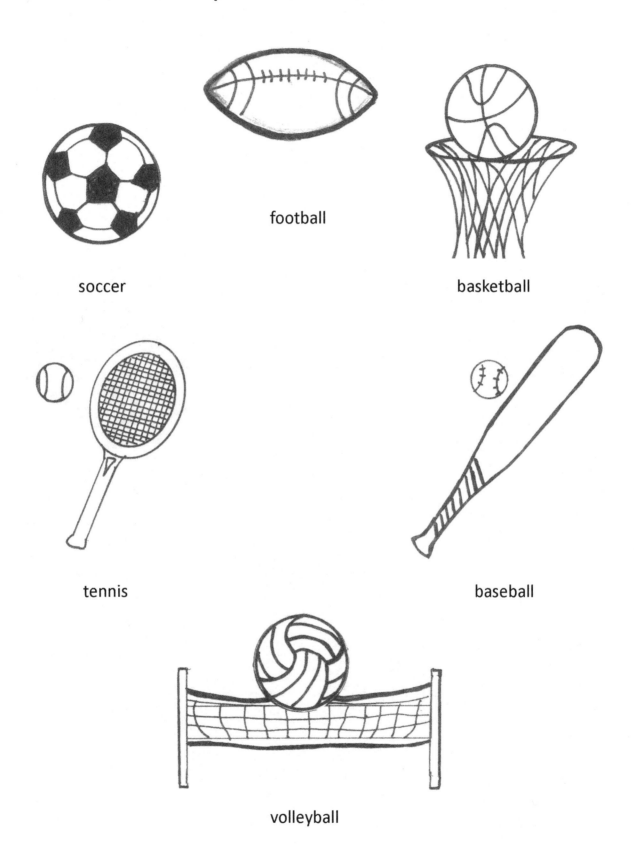

soccer

football

basketball

tennis

baseball

volleyball

Sports and Recreation

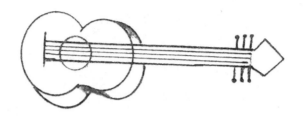

the guitar

cards

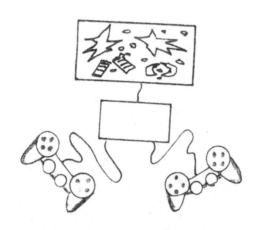

checkers

video games

Label the Pictures

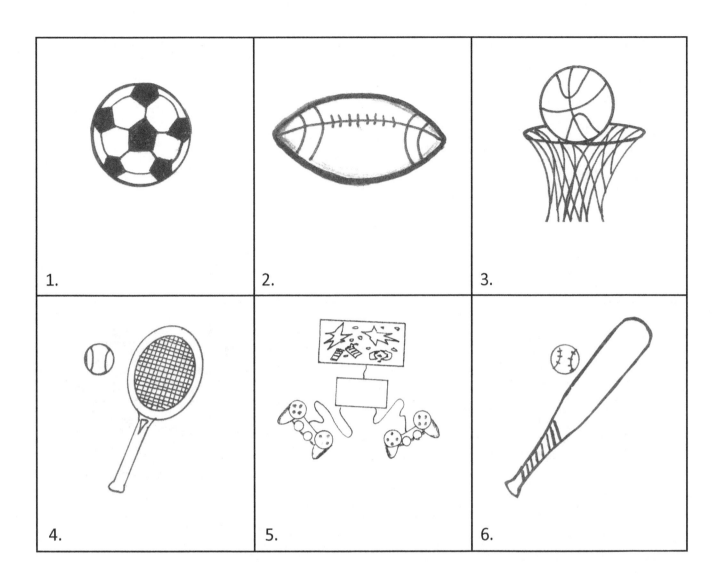

1.
2.
3.
4.
5.
6.

Answer Box	
baseball	(the) guitar
basketball	soccer
cards	tennis
checkers	video games
football	volleyball

Label the Pictures

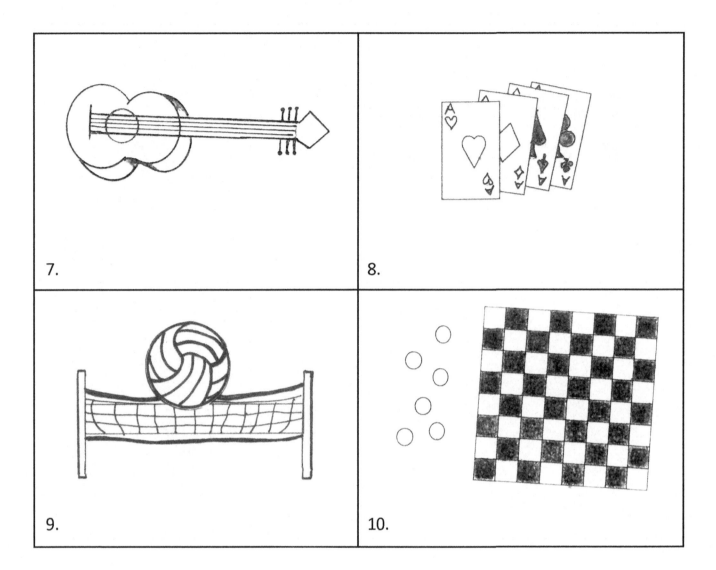

7.

8.

9.

10.

Answer Box	
baseball	(the) guitar
basketball	soccer
cards	tennis
checkers	video games
football	volleyball

Sports: Pictures to Sentences

Examples: **I am** playing football.   **She is** playing football.
          They are playing football.   **He is** playing football.

Directions: Look at the picture and tell what the person is playing.

	1. What is **John** playing? **He is** playing football.
	2. What are **you** playing?
	3. What are **they** playing?
	4. What is **Joe** playing?
	5. What is **Mary** playing?

Sports: Pictures to Sentences

	6. What are **John and Mary** playing?
	7. What is **Dad** playing?
	8. What are **you** playing?
	9. What is your **brother** playing?
	10. What are your **friends** playing?

Sports Sentences

I	*		soccer.
You			football.
He			video games.
She			tennis.
We	*am		cards.
They		playing	basketball.
John and Susan	*are		baseball.
My father			volleyball.
My mother	*is		checkers.
My sister			
My brothers			
My friends			

Directions: Write 18 sentences using this chart. Take words from each box to form sentences.

* Remember: * I **am** * You **are** *He **is** * She **is** *We **are** *They **are**

1. **I am** playing baseball. _____

2. **You are** playing baseball. _____

3. **He is** playing baseball. _____

4. **She is** playing baseball. _____

5. **We are** playing baseball. _____

6. **They are** playing baseball. _____

7. _____

Sports Sentences

8. _____

9. _____

10._____

11._____

12._____

13._____

14._____

15._____

16._____

17._____

18._____

19._____

20._____

21._____

22._____

23._____

24._____

Directions: Find a partner. Take turns reading your sentences to each other.

Summer Sports Camp

Directions: Read the story.

Yippee! Chuck and his friends are very happy. It is the first week of Summer Sports Camp. They are going to play sports all day long for two weeks! They are going to play soccer, football, baseball, basketball, tennis, and volleyball. During free time, they can play other fun things like video games, checkers, or cards. At night, they are going to sit around a bonfire and sing songs and listen to the camp counselor play the guitar. The best part is when they listen to the counselor's stories. Some stories are funny and some are scary. Chuck likes the scary stories.

On the first day of camp, Chuck and Juan choose soccer. Ben chooses football. Lee chooses tennis. Joe chooses baseball, and Dave chooses basketball. No one chooses volleyball.

It is a good day so far. Juan is happy because he makes a goal. Dave makes three baskets, so he is happy, too. Joe is a fast pitcher, so his team is happy.

The boys play quiet games during free time. Ben and Lee play video games. Dave and Juan play cards. Joe and Chuck play checkers.

At night, the boys roast marshmallows on a stick and listen to their counselor, Tim. Tim plays the guitar and sings. After that, he tells funny stories about things at the camp. Tomorrow he will tell scary stories.

Chuck is so happy! He feels so lucky. He gets to spend two weeks with his best friends and have two weeks of fun! Chuck thinks that he will never forget Summer Sports Camp!

1-6 (B):

Summer Sports Camp: Questions (1-7)

Directions: Read the story and answer the questions with complete sentences.

1. Name the six sports that the boys are going to play.

_____

_____

2. What can the boys play during free time?

_____

_____

3. Which sport does Dave choose?

_____

_____

4. Why is Dave happy?

_____

_____

5. Which sport does Juan choose?

_____

_____

6. Why is Juan happy?

_____

_____

7. Which game does Joe choose?

_____

_____

Summer Sports Camp: Questions (8-14)

8. Why is Joe's team happy?

_____

_____

9. Who plays video games?

_____

_____

10. Who plays checkers?

_____

_____

11. Who plays cards?

_____

_____

12. Who plays the guitar?

_____

_____

13. Who tells funny stories?

_____

_____

14. Why is Chuck so happy?

_____

_____

Summer Sports Camp: Questions (15-16)

15.	Who thinks he will never forget Summer Sports Camp?

_____

_____

16.	Write about a time when you went to a summer camp. Tell about the things you enjoyed doing at camp. Talk about your fun.

								or

	Write about one summer when you had a very good time with your friends. Tell about the things that you enjoyed. Talk about your fun.

_____

_____

_____

_____

_____

_____

_____

_____

Directions: Find a partner. Read your stories to each other.

More Sports and Recreation

swimming

skateboarding

riding a bike

fishing

More Sports and Recreation

skating

skiing

running / jogging

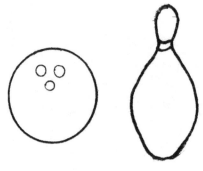

bowling

Label the Pictures

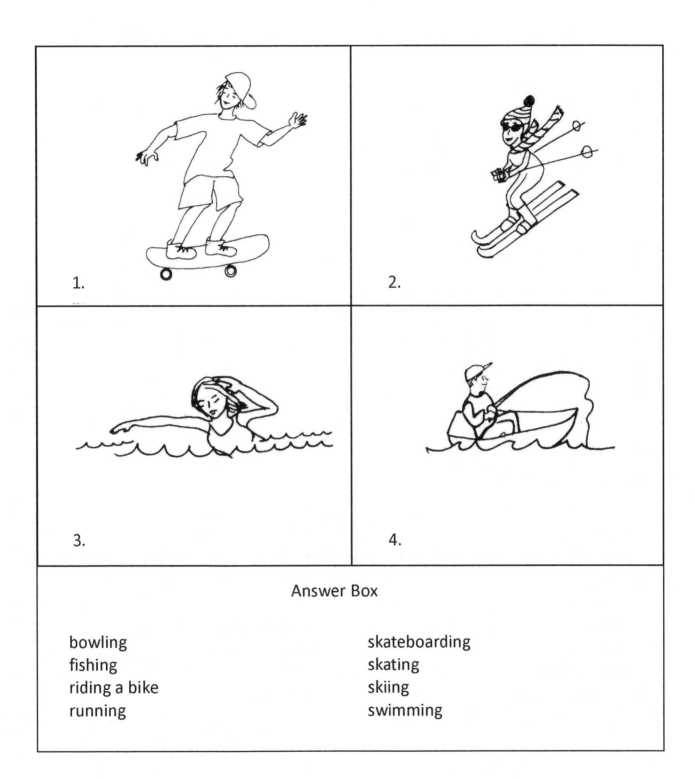

1.

2.

3.

4.

Answer Box

bowling   skateboarding
fishing   skating
riding a bike   skiing
running   swimming

Label the Pictures

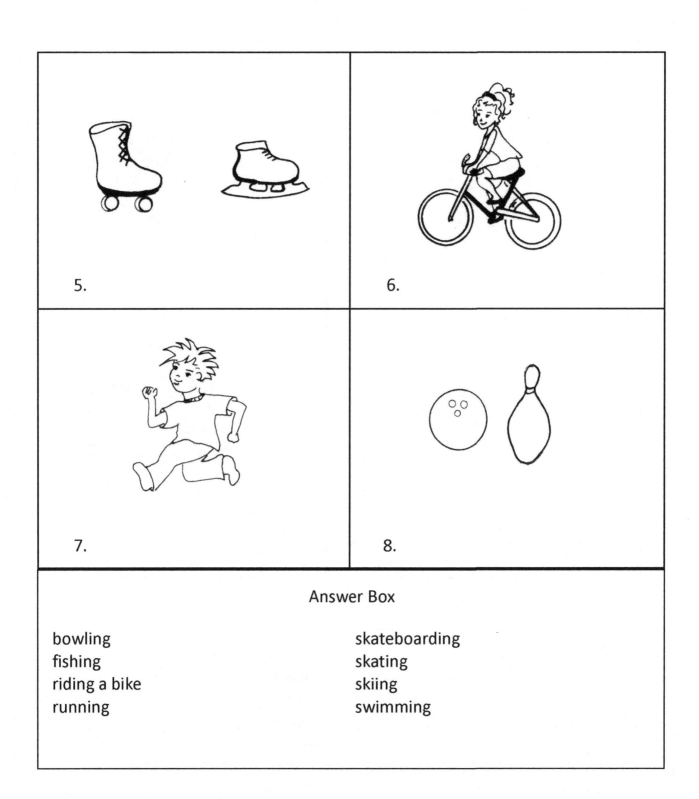

5.

6.

7.

8.

Answer Box

bowling   skateboarding
fishing   skating
riding a bike   skiing
running   swimming

Pictures to Sentences

Directions: Look at the picture and complete the sentence by filling in the blank. Then, rewrite the whole sentence.

	1. He is _____**fishing**_____. **He is fishing.**
	2. I am _____.
	3. You are _____.
	4. They are _____.

Pictures to Sentences

	5. She is _____.
	6. We are _____.
	7. He is _____.
	8. I am _____.

Writing Sentences: More Sports and Recreation

Directions: Use this chart to write 10 sentences.

* Remember: I **am**   You **are**   He **is**   She **is**   We **are**   They **are**

	*	
I You He She We They Joe Sara My sister My friend My friends My brother My cousins My father My mother	*am *are *is	swimming. skating. bike riding. fishing. skateboarding. skiing. running. bowling.

Examples:

1. _____ *I am* running _____ .

2. _____ *You are* running _____ .

3. _____ *He is* running _____ .

4. _____ *They are* running _____ .

5. _____ *We are* running _____ .

Writing Sentences: More Sports and Recreation

6. _____

7. _____

8. _____

9. _____

10. _____

11. _____

12. _____

13. _____

14. _____

15. _____

Directions: Write your own sentences. Use names or activities that you want.

_____

_____

_____

_____

_____

_____

_____

Writing Questions: More Sports and Recreation

Directions: Use this chart to write 12 questions.

* Remember: * **Am I**   ***Are you**   ***Is he** ***Is she**   ***Are we**   ***Are they**

*	I	swimming?
	you	skating?
	he	bike riding?
*Am	she	fishing?
*Are	we	skateboarding?
*Is	they	skiing?
	my friends	running?
	my father	bowling?
	my mother	playing soccer?
	my brother	playing football?
	my sister	playing baseball?
	my friend	playing video games?
		playing cards?

Examples:

1. _____ *Am I skateboarding* _____ ?

2. _____ *Are you skateboarding* _____ ?

3. _____ *Is he skateboarding* _____ ?

4. _____ *Is she skateboarding* _____ ?

5. _____ *Is my brother skateboarding* _____ ?

6. _____ *Are they skateboarding* _____ ?

7. _____ *Are we skateboarding* _____ ?

Writing Questions: More Sports and Recreation

8. <u>Are my friends skateboarding</u> _____ ?

9. _____

10. _____

11. _____

12. _____

13. _____

14. _____

15. _____

16. _____

17. _____

18. _____

19. _____

20. _____

Summer Vacation

It is the first month of summer vacation. I am having fun. My friends are having fun, too. Everyone is doing something different. This is what my girlfriends are doing. Sandra is riding a bike. Mary is jogging. Linda is skating. Janet and Molly are playing tennis. Sometimes I play with them.

The boys that I go to school with are having fun, too. Mario is playing soccer. Tom is playing football. Sam is playing basketball. Jerry is skateboarding.

Even my family is having fun. We are at the beach for one week. Dad is fishing. Mother is playing mini-golf. My sisters are playing volleyball on the beach. My brothers are water skiing. In the winter they like to go skiing in the snow. I am swimming. I love summer vacation. There are so many things to do when I'm on vacation!

Questions

Directions: Read the story and answer the questions in complete sentences.

* Remember, sometimes the sentences start with **"He is," "She is," "They are,"** and **"You are."**

1. What is Linda doing?
   She is skating.

2. What is Sandra doing?

3. What is Mary doing?

4. Who is skating?

Summer Vacation – Questions

5. What are Janet and Molly doing?

6. What is Jerry doing?

7. Who is playing football?

8. Who is playing soccer?

9. What is Sam doing?

10. What is Dad doing?

11. What is Mom doing?

12. Who is playing volleyball?

13. What are my brothers doing?

14. What am I doing?

Summer Vacation: Matching Sentences to Pictures

Directions: Look at the pictures. Read the story. **Find the sentences** in the story that **go with the pictures. Write the sentences** next to the pictures.

(jogging)	**1. Mary is jogging.**
(riding a bike)	2.
(playing tennis)	3.
(skating)	4.

Summary Vacation: Matching Sentences to Pictures

(skateboarding)	5.
(playing soccer)	6.
(playing basketball)	7.
(playing football)	8.

Summer Vacation: Matching Sentences to Pictures

 (swimming)	9.
 (playing volleyball)	10.
 (fishing)	11.

Three Stories about Me

Word Box

bowl	play cards
fish	play checkers
ride a bike	play chess
skate	play baseball
skateboard	play basketball
ski	play football
swim	play soccer
	play tennis
	play the guitar
	play video games
	play volleyball

Story #1 (Example)

Hi. I'm _____Jane_____. When I have time to play and relax, I

__swim_____, or I _____ride my bike_____. This is fun for me. This is

what I do in my free time.

Your Story

Hi. I'm _____. When I have time to play and relax, I

_____, or

I _____.

This is fun for me. This is what I do in my free time.

Three Stories about Me

Story #2 (Example)

Hi. My name is ___*Tom*___. I know how to ___*play football*___,

___*ride a bike*___, and ___*play video games*___. I don't know how to

___*skateboard*___, ___*play chess*___, or ___*play the guitar*___.

I want to learn how to ___*skateboard*___.

Your Story #2

Hi. My name is _____. I know how to _____,

_____, and _____.

I don't know how to _____, _____,

or _____. I want to learn how to _____.

Your Story #3

Directions: Write a story about what you do in your free time. Then get a partner and read the three stories to each other.

_____

_____

_____

_____

_____

_____

Sports and Recreation: Quiz #1

Directions: Label the pictures.

1.	2.	3.
4.	5.	6.

Answer Box

baseball
basketball
cards
football
(the) guitar
soccer

Sports and Recreation: Quiz #2

Directions: Label the pictures.

1.

2.

3.

4.

5.

6.

Answer Box

bowling
fishing
riding a bike
running / jogging
skating
swimming

Sports and Recreation: Quiz #3

Directions: Answer each question with a complete sentence.

1. What is Joe playing?   (football)

2. What is Mrs. Green playing? (tennis)

3. What are we playing?   (basketball)

4. What are they playing? (baseball)

5. What are you playing? (soccer)

6. What is Mr. Green doing? (bowling)

7. What am I doing? (swimming)

8. What are Sam and Jim doing? (skating)

Chapter #2

Possessive Adjectives

Possessive Adjectives

Possessive adjectives such as "**my**," "**your**," "**his**," "**her**," "**his**," "**its**," "**our**," and "**their**" show ownership.   Examples:

I – *my*	I am brushing *my* teeth.
You – *your*	**You** are brushing *your* teeth.
He – *his*	**He** is brushing *his* teeth.
She – *her*	**She** is brushing *her* teeth.
It – *its*	**It** is brushing *its* teeth.
We – *our*	**We** are brushing *our* teeth.
They – *their*	**They** are brushing *their* teeth.

Directions: Fill in the blank with the correct possessive adjective: "**my**," "**your**," "**his**," "**her**," "**his**," "**its**," "**our**," or "**their**"

1. **I** am washing _____**my**_____ hands.

2. **He** is washing _____hands.

3. **You** are washing _____hands.

4. **She** is washing _____hands.

5. **We** are washing _____hands.

6. **It** is washing _____paws.

7. **They** are washing _____hands.

8. **She** is eating _____breakfast.

9. **You** are eating _____lunch.

10. **I** am eating _____dinner.

11. **They** are cleaning _____yard.

12. **It** is eating _____food.

13. **He** is talking to _____son.

14. **We** are painting _____house.

15. **They** are washing _____clothes.

16. **I** am putting on _____make up.

17. **You** are washing _____face.

18. **He** is washing _____car.

19. **She** is brushing _____hair.

20. **I** am polishing _____nails.

21. **He** is looking for _____wallet.

22. **She** is looking for _____keys.

Substitute the Underlined Words
with a Possessive Adjective

Directions: Rewrite the sentences and use a possessive adjective ("**his,**" "**her,**" "**its,**" "**their**") in place of the underlined word.

Example: Mary is brushing _**Mary's**_ teeth.

Mary is brushing ___**her**___ teeth.

1. Joe is washing _**Joe's**_ hands.

2. The dog is licking _**the dog's**_ paws.

3. Bob is riding _**Bob's**_ bike.

4. My sister, Sara, is cleaning _**Sara's**_ room.

5. Father is waxing _**Father's**_ car.

6. Mother is polishing _**Mother's**_ nails.

7. My brother, Henry, is washing _**Henry's**_ jeans.

Substitute the Underlined Words
With a Possessive Adjective

Directions: Rewrite each sentence and use a possessive adjective (**"his," "her," "its,"**
"their") in place of the underlined word.

8. Bill and Irma are finishing ***Bill's and Irma's*** homework.

9. Mr. and Mrs. Smith are swimming in ***Mr. and Mrs. Smith's*** pool.

10. Mary is brushing ***Mary's*** hair.

11. Joe is washing ***Joe's*** hands.

12. Juan is combing ***Juan's*** hair.

13. Mrs. Smith is putting on ***Mrs. Smith's*** coat.

14. Mr. Smith is wearing ***Mr. Smith's*** new tie.

15. The twins are putting away **the twins'** toys.

Writing Sentences with Possessive Adjectives

(A) Directions: Write 8 sentences using the chart.   Choose the proper form:

  *   I-**my**   he-**his**   you-**your**   she-**her**

I am		*	book bag.
You are	looking for	**my**	pencil.
He is		**your**	ruler.
She is		**his**	book.
My sister is		**her**	markers.
My brother is			eraser.
Mrs. Smith is			stapler.

Example: I am looking for **my** eraser.

1._____

2._____

3._____

4._____

5._____

6._____

7._____

8._____

Writing Sentences with Possessive Adjectives

(B) Directions: Write 9 sentences using this chart. Choose the proper form:

* they-**their**   we-**our**

We are They are Bob and Bill are Bob and I are My friends and I are Mr. and Mrs. Garza are	washing	* our their	clothes. jeans. towels. socks. uniforms. tee shirts.

Example: <u>We</u> are washing **our** towels.

1._____

2._____

3._____

4._____

5._____

6._____

7._____

8._____

9._____

Let's Say It! – Oral Practice Review:
I-my he-his she-her it-its you-your we-our they-their

Directions: Choose a partner. Practice asking and answering the questions.

A. What is Mom doing?
B. She is washing her _____*_____.

(*blouse *skirt *dress *hair *face)

Examples: Repeat the whole question and whole answer for each substitution.

A. What is Mom doing?
B. She is washing her **_blouse_**.

A. What is Mom doing?
B. She is washing her **_skirt._**

A. What is Mom doing?
B. She is washing her **_dress_**.

A. What is Mom doing?
B. She is washing her **_hair_**.

A. What is Mom doing?
B. She is washing her **_face_**.

1. A. What is Dad doing?
   B. He is putting away his _____*_____.

   (* shoes * pants * tie * socks * suit)

Let's Say It! – Oral Practice Review:
I-my he-his she-her it-its you-your we-our they-their

2. A. What are you doing?
   B. I am doing my _____ * _____.

   (*math homework   *English homework *exercises *chores *laundry)

3. A. What are your neighbors doing?
   B. They are painting their _____ * _____.

   (*kitchen   *dining room *bedroom *living room *house)

4. A. What are you and your family doing?
   B. We are cleaning our _____ * _____.

   (*house *apartment *kitchen *basement *garage *yard)

Can you make up a dialogue?

5. A._____?

   B. _____.

   (   )

Possessive Adjectives: Quiz #1

Directions: Fill in the blanks with possessive adjectives: **my, your, his, her, its, our, their.**

1. <u>Mrs. Jones</u> is praising _____her_____ hard-working students.

2. My <u>uncle</u> is painting _____ house.

3. My <u>dog</u> is looking for _____ bone.

4. <u>I</u> am doing _____ homework.

5. My <u>friends</u> are choosing me to be on _____ team.

6. My <u>dad</u> is eating _____ breakfast.

7. The <u>neighbors</u> are painting _____ porch.

8. <u>We</u> are doing _____ science project.

9. My <u>sister</u> is washing _____ shorts and tee shirts.

10. My little <u>brothers</u> are picking up _____toys.

11. <u>Mrs. Jones</u> is saying nice things about _____ students.

12. <u>You</u> are taking _____ driving test today.

13. <u>We</u> are doing _____ best in school.

14. <u>He</u> is talking to _____ girlfriend.

15. <u>She</u> is talking to _____ husband.

16. My <u>brother</u> is washing _____ motorcycle.

17. <u>Dad</u> is fixing _____ truck.

18. <u>You</u> are writing _____ own sentences.

19. My <u>cat</u> is licking _____ paws.

20. <u>You</u> are taking _____ brother to the dentist.

21. <u>I</u> am doing _____ exercises.

22. <u>You</u> are brushing _____ hair.

23. <u>She</u> is brushing _____ teeth.

24. <u>He</u> is combing _____ hair.

25. <u>We</u> are riding _____ bikes.

26. <u>They</u> are listening to _____ teacher.

27. <u>I</u> am listening to _____ teacher.

28. <u>He</u> is listening to _____ teacher.

Possessive Adjectives: Quiz #2

Directions: Write 12 sentences using the possessive adjectives: **my, your, his, her, its, our, their.**

1._____*They are painting their house.*_____

2._____

3._____

4._____

5._____

6._____

7._____

8._____

9._____

10._____

11._____

12._____

13._____

Chapter #3

Overview
of
The Simple Present Tense

With Spelling Practice Worksheets for Verbs Ending in "s" and "es" and "ies"

The Simple Present – Overview

Use the Simple Present when you want to talk about something that you do **regularly,** for example: every morning, every day, every afternoon, every night, every weekend, every Saturday, every month, every year, *etc*.

Use the Simple Present to talk about **routines.**

Use the Simple Present to talk about **facts.**

The Simple Present - Overview: Affirmative

1. The **Simple Present Affirmative** is formed like this: **Subject   +   Verb.**

The **important** thing to remember is that there is an **"s"** on the *verb* when it is used with **"he," "she,"** or **"it."**

Examples:

Subject	+	Verb
I		play.
You		play.
He		play<u>s</u>.
She		play<u>s</u>.
It		play<u>s</u>.
We		play.
You		play.
They		play.

The Simple Present - Overview: Negative

2. The **Simple Present Negative** is formed like this:

Subject   +   do <u>not</u> / does <u>not</u>   +   Verb

or

Subject   +   don't / doesn't   +   Verb

Put **"*not*"** after **"do"** or **"does"** or use the abbreviations **"don't"** or **"doesn't."**

* **"Don't"** is the abbreviation for **"do not."**
* **"Doesn't"** is the abbreviation for **"does not."**

Examples:

S +	do not / does not	+ Verb		S +	don't / doesn't	+ Verb
I	**do *not***	like	pizza.	I	**don't**	like pizza.
You	**do *not***	like	pizza.	You	**don't**	like pizza.
He	**does *not***	like	pizza.	He	**doesn't**	like pizza.
She	**does *not***	like	pizza.	She	**doesn't**	like pizza.
It	**does *not***	like	pizza.	It	**doesn't**	like pizza.
We	**do *not***	like	pizza.	We	**don't**	like pizza.
You	**do *not***	like	pizza.	You	**don't**	like pizza.
They	**do *not***	like	pizza.	They	**don't**	like pizza

The Simple Present – Overview
Questions

3. **Simple Present Questions** are formed like this:

Do / Does + Subject + Verb   ?

Examples:

Do / Does	+	Subject	+	Verb	
Do		I		like	candy?
Do		you		like	candy?
Does		he		like *	candy?
Does		she		like *	candy?
Does		it		like *	candy?
Do		we		like	candy?
Do		you		like	candy?
Do		they		like	candy?

* Notice there is no **"s"** on the main verb because the **"s"** is already on the helping verb "does."

The Simple Present – Overview:
Spelling Rules: Adding "s" to Verbs

The **Simple Present Affirmative** requires that **"s"** be placed at the **end of the verb** when used with **"he," "she,"** or **"it."**

Examples:

I eat breakfast.	We eat breakfast.
You eat breakfast.	You eat breakfast.
He **eats** breakfast.	They eat breakfast.
She **eats** breakfast.	
It **eats** breakfast.	

Most of the time an **"s"** is simply added to the end of the verb, and other times an **"es"** or **"ies"** is added. The following is a quick review of five rules:

1. Just add **"s"** to the verb.

Clean - cleans	Fight - fights
Cook - cooks	Get - gets
Drink - drinks	Play - plays
Eat - eats	Talk - talks
Feel - feels	Work - works

2. For verbs ending in **"e,"** just add **"s."**

Bake - bakes	Live - lives
Bite - bites	Make - makes
Dance - dances	Ride - rides
Give - gives	Take - takes
Like - likes	Write - writes

The Simple Present - Overview
Spelling Rules: Adding "s" to Verbs

3. For verbs ending in **"ch," "sh," "ss," "x,"** add **"es."**

Brush - brushes	Reach - reaches
Catch - catches	Rush - rushes
Dress - dresses	Teach - teaches
Fix - fixes	Wash - washes
Kiss - kisses	Watch - watches

4. For verbs ending in a consonant and a **"y,"** drop the **"y,"** and add **"ies."**

Carry - carries	Hurry - hurries
Cry - cries	Study - studies
Dry - dries	Try - tries
Fly - flies	Worry - worries

5. **"Do," "go,"** and **"have"** are irregular verbs. Their spellings have to be memorized.

Do - does
Go - goes
Have - has

Spelling Practice Worksheet #1:
Practice the Spelling Rule for Adding "s"

Directions: Add **"s"** to the following verbs.

Example: Clean - clean*s*	5. Fight -
1. Cook -	6. Get -
2. Drink -	7. Play -
3. Eat -	8. Talk -
4. Feel -	9. Work -

Directions: Rewrite the sentences with the **"s"** form of the verb.

1. He (clean) his room every Saturday.

*He **cleans** his room every Saturday*_____.

2. She (cook) dinner every night.

_____.

3. It (drink) water.

_____.

4. He (eat) breakfast every morning.

_____.

Practice the Spelling Rule for Adding "s"

5. My sister (feel) sick.

   _____.

6. The dog (fight) with the cat.

   _____.

7. My little brother (get) an ice cream cone every Saturday.

   _____.

8. Jack (play) basketball every day after school.

   _____.

9. He (talk) to his girlfriend every day.

   _____.

10. My dad (work) in construction.

   _____.

11. She (look) very happy.

   _____.

Directions: Write 3 of your own sentences. Then choose a partner and read the 14 sentences to each other.

   _____.

   _____.

   _____.

Spelling Practice Worksheet #2:
Practice the Spelling Rule for Adding "es"

Directions: Add **"es"** to verbs ending in **"ch," "sh," "ss,"** and **"x."**

1. Brush -	7. Reach -
2. Catch -	8. Rush -
3. Dress -	9. Teach -
4. Fix -	10. Wash -
5. Kiss -	11. Watch -
6. Polish -	

Directions: Rewrite the sentences with the **"s"** form of the verb by adding **"es"** to the verb.

1. Mrs. Turner (teach) English in the middle school.

*Mrs. Turner teach**es** English in the middle school*   .

2. He (brush) his teeth every morning.

_____.

3. The mother (kiss) her baby.

_____.

Practice the Spelling Rule for Adding "es"

4. My dad (polish) his shoes every Sunday.

_____.

5. My aunt (dress) up to go to lunch with her friends.

_____.

6. He (reach) for the baseball and (catch) it.

_____.

7. My cousin (watch) too much TV.

_____.

8. My brother (rush) to catch the school bus every morning.

_____.

9. Mom (wash) the clothes every Saturday.

_____.

10. My uncle (fix) cars.

_____.

Directions: Write 2 of your own sentences. Choose a partner and take turns reading the 12 sentences to each other.

_____.

_____.

Spelling Practice Worksheet #3:
Practice the Spelling Rule for Adding "ies"

For verbs ending in a consonant and "**y**," drop the "**y**," and add "**ies.**"

Example: Carry - carr**ies**	4. Hurry -
1. Cry -	5. Study -
2. Dry -	6. Try -
3. Fly -	7. Worry -

Directions: Rewrite the sentences with the "**s**" form of the verb. Do this by dropping the "**y**" and adding "**ies.**"

1. She (study) very hard.

*She stud**ies** very hard*   .

2. Jose (carry) the grocery bags for his mother.

_____.

3. She (dry) her hands with a towel.

_____.

4. My aunt (cry) during sad movies.

_____.

5. My uncle (fly) to Texas once a month.

_____.

63

Practice the Spelling Rule for Adding "ies"

6. Mrs. Cantor (worry) about her sick neighbor.

_____.

7. The dog (bury) the bone in the backyard.

_____.

8. Mom (fry) the chicken in that pan.

_____.

9. My sister (study) every night.

_____.

10. He always (try) his best.

_____.

11. The movie is about a princess who (marry) a poor man.

_____.

12. Little brother (hurry) to catch up with big brother.

_____.

Directions: Write 2 of your own sentences. Then choose a partner and read them to each other.

_____.

_____.

Spelling Practice Worksheet #4:
Practice the Spelling Rule for Adding "s" to Verbs Ending in "e"

Add **"s"** to verbs ending with **"e."**

Example: Bake - *bakes*	5. Live -
1. Bite -	6. Make -
2. Dance -	7. Ride -
3. Give -	8. Take -
4. Like -	9. Write -

Directions: Rewrite the sentences with the **"s"** form of the verb.

1. Mom (make) chocolate chip cookies every Friday.

Mom makes chocolate chip cookies every Friday   .

2. The dog (bite) his toy bone.

_____.

3. She (dance) with John.

_____.

4. He (drive) a red truck.

_____.

5. My mother (give) me lunch money.

_____.

Practice the Spelling Rule for Adding "s" to Verbs Ending in "e"

6. My friend (like) to play baseball.

_____.

7. Sue (invite) us to her birthday party every year.

_____.

8. Bob (live) close to me.

_____.

9. She (make) the most delicious cakes.

_____.

10. My cousin (ride) his bike to school.

_____.

11. Grandmother (take) her medicine every morning.

_____.

12. He (write) novels.

_____.

Directions: Write 2 of your own sentences.

_____.

_____.

Directions: Choose a partner and read all of the sentences to each other.

Spelling Practice Worksheet #5:
Practice the Spelling Rule for Irregular Verbs

Notice that irregular verbs require that you remember the **"s"** form of the verb. No particular rules apply, so you just have to memorize them.

> Do - does
> Go - goes
> Have - has

Directions: Rewrite the sentences with the **"s"** form of the verb.

Example: My sister (do) her homework before she watches television.
My sister does her homework before she watches television   .

1. My brother (do) his homework before he plays video games.

_____.

2. My mother (do) her exercises before she (go) to bed.

_____.

3. She (go) to college in Florida.

_____.

4. He (go) to work at 9 o'clock.

_____.

5. The baby (have) a fever.

_____.

6. She (have) two children.

_____.

7. My dad (have) two jobs.

_____.

Spelling Review

Directions: Write the **"s"** form of the verb by adding **"s,"** **"es,"** or **"ies"** to the verbs. Look at your practice pages for help. Verbs are in alphabetical order for easy reference.

1. Bake - *bakes*	10. Dance -
2. Bite -	11. Do -
3. Brush -	12. Dress -
4. Bury -	13. Drink -
5. Carry -	14. Drive -
6. Catch -	15. Dry -
7. Clean -	16. Eat -
8. Cook -	17. Feel -
9. Cry -	18. Fight -

Spelling Review

Directions: Write the **"s"** form of the verb.

19. Fix - *fixes*	34. Play -
20. Fly -	35. Polish -
21. Fry -	36. Reach -
22. Get -	37. Ride -
23. Go -	38. Rush -
24. Give -	39. Study -
25. Have -	40. Take -
26. Hurry -	41. Talk -
27. Invite -	42. Teach -
28. Kiss -	43. Try -
29. Like -	44. Walk -
30. Live -	45. Wash -
31. Look -	46. Watch -
32. Make -	47. Worry -
33. Miss -	48. Write -

Chapter #4

Simple Present Tense - Affirmative

Simple Present Affirmative:
Choosing the Correct Form of the Verb

The **Simple Present Affirmative** is formed like this: **Subject + Verb.** The important thing to remember with the affirmative is that there is an **"s"** at the end of the verb when it is used with **"he," "she,"** and **"it."**

Subject + Verb

I	play.
You	play.
He	play**s**.
She	play**s**.
It	play**s**.
We	play.
You	play.
They	play.

Directions: Choose the correct form of the verb: **play** or **plays**.

play or plays

1. I_____golf.

2. You_____basketball.

3. He_____football.

4. She_____volleyball.

5. It_____catch.

6. We_____soccer.

7. They_____baseball.

4-1: Continued

Directions: Choose the correct form of the verb.

drink or **drinks**

8. I _____ tea.

9. You _____ lemonade.

10. She _____ coffee.

11. He _____ milk.

12. It _____ water.

13. We _____ juice.

14. They _____ sodas.

eat or **eats**

15. They_____pizza.

16. He_____hamburgers.

17. I_____sandwiches.

18. She_____salads.

19. You_____spaghetti.

20. We_____hot dogs.

21. It_____meat.

22. My dog_____dog food.

23. Jerry and Joe_____tacos.

24. Sandra_____vegetables.

25. Nancy and I_____fruit.

26. Tan_____egg rolls.

27. Mr. Spot_____cake.

28. Mrs. Spot_____pie.

4-1: Continued

Directions: Choose the correct form of the verb.

live or lives

29. I_____in Washington, D. C.

30. My sister _____in New York.

31. My parents_____in Houston.

32. My brother_____in Los Angeles.

33. We _____in an apartment.

34. They _____in a house.

35. The bird _____in a tree.

36. You _____close to me.

study or studies

37. They_____English.

38. We_____Spanish.

39. You_____French.

40. I_____computer programming.

41. Mark_____air conditioning repair.

42. Lucy_____cosmetology.

43. She_____nursing.

44. Bill_____auto mechanics.

fix or fixes

45. I_____cars.

46. He_____trucks.

47. You_____motorcycles.

48. She_____bicycles.

Simple Present Affirmative:
Changing Sentences: Change "I" to "He"

Remember that **"he,"** **"she,"** and **"it"** take an **"s"** on the verb.

Examples:

Subject	Verb	
I	eat	breakfast.
You	eat	breakfast.
He	eat**s**	breakfast.
She	eat**s**	breakfast.
It	eat**s**	breakfast.
We	eat	breakfast.
You	eat	breakfast.
They	eat	breakfast.

Directions: Rewrite the sentences changing **"I"** to **"He."** Also, change **"my"** to **"his."**

1. I get up early.

 He gets up early   .

2. I get up at 6:30.

 He gets up at 6:30   .

3. I brush <u>my</u> teeth.

_____.

4. I shave.

_____.

Changing Sentences: Change "I" to "He"

5. I take a shower.

_____

6. I get dressed.

_____

7. I drink coffee.

_____

8. I eat eggs for breakfast.

_____

9. I get my lunch.

_____

10. I go to work.

_____

11. I work very hard all day.

_____

12. Then I come back home.

_____

Directions: Choose a partner. Take turns with you and your partner reading the sentences with "I" and then with "He."

Sally's Morning Routine

Directions: Read the story below. Each line in the story is numbered so you can find it easily on the next page.

        Hi. My name is Sally. This is what I do every morning.

1. I get up at 6:30.

2. I go to the bathroom.

3. I brush my teeth.

4. I take a shower.

5. I wash my hair.

6. I dry myself.

7. I put on my clothes.

8. I brush my hair and fix it.

9. I go to the kitchen.

10. I drink orange juice.

11. I eat cereal.

12. I get my book bag.

13. I get my lunch.

14. I go outside.

15. I walk to school with my friends.

This Is What Sally Does
Every Morning

Directions: Rewrite the story using **"she."** Start every sentence with **"She."**

* Remember to change the pronoun **"my"** to **"her."** Also remember that the verb needs an **"s"** when used with **"he," "she,"** or **"it."**

1. She **gets** up at 6:30 _____.

2. _____.

3. _____.

4. _____.

5. _____.

6. _____.

7. _____.

8. _____.

9. _____.

10. _____.

11. _____.

12. _____.

13. _____.

14. _____.

15. _____.

Simple Present: Matching Pictures to Sentences

Directions: Go back and read the story "Sally's Morning Routine." Find the sentence that matches the picture. Write the sentence next to the picture that matches it.

	1. I get up at 6:30.
	2.
	3.
	4.

Simple Present: Matching Pictures to Sentences

	5.
	6.
	7.
	8.

My Morning Routine

Directions: Write what YOU do every morning.

_____

_____

_____

_____

_____

_____

_____

_____

_____

_____

_____

_____

My Mom's Morning Routine

Directions: Write what your mother does every morning.

Mother gets up at 5:00 every morning. _____

_____

_____

_____

_____

_____

_____

_____

_____

Directions: Choose a partner. Read what YOU do every morning and what your MOM does every morning. Then listen to your partner's stories.

After School

Directions: Read the story about what Bill does after school.

Hi. My name is Bill. This is what I do every day after school.

1. I get home from school at 3:00.
2. I take off my good school clothes.
3. I put on my play clothes.
4. I go to the kitchen.
5. I make a cheese sandwich or a peanut butter sandwich.
6. I drink orange juice.
7. I turn on the TV.
8. I watch cartoons.
9. I rest for a little while.
10. I ride my bike to the park.
11. I play basketball with my friends.
12. I go back home.
13. I play video games with my brother.
14. I help Mom get dinner ready.
15. I eat dinner.
16. I wash dishes.
17. I do my homework.
18. I go to bed at 9:00.

Directions: Answer the following questions in complete sentences.

Example: What time does Bill get home?
Bill gets home at 3:00.

1. What does Bill make to eat?

2. What does Bill drink?

After School

3. What does Bill watch on TV?

4. Where does Bill ride his bike to?

5. What does Bill play with his friends?

6. What does Bill play with his brother?

7. Who does Bill help?

8. What does Bill wash?

9. What does Bill do before he goes to bed?

My After School Routine

Directions: Now write about what YOU do after school.

Hi. My name is _____. This is what I do every day after school.

_____

_____

_____

_____

_____

_____

_____

_____

_____

_____

_____

Directions: Choose a partner. Read your stories to each other. Choose another partner. Read your stories to each other.

Frank Falls

Directions: Read the story then answer the questions that follow on the next page.

It is a sunny summer day. Frank is standing in his front yard. Suddenly, Frank hears something up in the tree. He looks up and sees his cat. His cat, Lolly, is in the tree and cannot get down. Frank quickly climbs the tree to get Lolly. A noisy car passes by and Frank looks. Lolly hisses, meows loudly, and scratches Frank. All of this causes Frank to fall!

Mother sees what happens and calls an ambulance. The ambulance takes Frank to the hospital. The doctor examines Frank. Frank has to stay in the hospital for a few days. Frank has a broken leg and other problems. Every day Frank asks Mom about Lolly. Every day Mom says that Lolly stays in Frank's room waiting for him to come home.

(Story continued on next page.)

Frank Falls (continued)

Sometimes Frank's leg hurts so much that Frank can't sleep. His nurse tells him to think of something that makes him happy. Frank thinks of Lolly, and he falls asleep.

Soon it is time to go home! The car pulls up to the house. Guess who runs to greet him? Lolly is purring and meowing with happiness! Lolly is rubbing against Frank's legs. Mom picks up Lolly so Frank doesn't slip and fall again. Frank knows he will get better very soon. He is with his friend, Lolly, the best kitty cat in the whole wide world! Soon he and Lolly will be playing again!

Questions about "Frank Falls"

Directions: Answer the questions about "Frank Falls" in complete sentences.

1. Why does Frank climb the tree?
His cat, Lolly, is in the tree and cannot get down. Frank climbs the tree to get his cat.

2. Why does Frank fall from the tree?

3. How does Frank get to the hospital?

4. Why can't Frank sleep at night?

Frank Falls

5. What does the nurse tell him to think about when he can't sleep?

6. What does Lolly do when she sees Frank?

7. What does Frank think about Lolly?

Directions: Choose (a) or (b) to write about. Draw a picture to go with your story.

(a) Write about a pet that you have or used to have, that you loved very much. Write the pet's name and some things that you used to do together.

or

(b) Write a paragraph about a time you hurt yourself.

_____

_____

_____

_____

_____

_____

_____

Directions: Choose a partner and read your stories to each other.

Dan's Saturday

Directions: Read "Dan's Saturday" and think about what *you* usually do on Saturdays.

Hi. My name is Dan. This is what I usually do on Saturday. I get up at 8 o'clock. I eat pancakes and drink apple juice. I watch cartoons. Then I make up my bed and take a shower. I get dressed. I go to the Shopping Plaza with my family. Mom buys things for us and for the house. Then we eat lunch at Yummy Burgers.

We come home, and I change into my play clothes.   I play basketball with my friends. I come back from the park, and I listen to music or read a scary book. I love scary books! Later, we all go visit Uncle George. Mom takes a big chocolate cake for dessert. We sit and eat a big dinner. After dinner, my Uncle George takes out his guitar, and we all sing. Soon, more relatives start dropping by. The grown-ups tell stories about each other. Everyone laughs and has fun. The children play video games or watch movies. We usually leave around 10 o'clock. We always have fun visiting Uncle George!

I am happy and tired when I get home. I fall asleep quickly. This is a regular Saturday for me.

Directions: Look at the next page and write your own story.

My Saturday

Directions: Now write about what *you* do on a Saturday.

Hi. My name is _____. This is what I usually do on Saturday. _____

_____

_____

_____

_____

_____

_____

_____

_____

_____

_____

_____

_____

_____

_____

_____

_____

_____

Directions: Choose a partner and read your stories to each other.

Extra Practice: Dan's Saturday

Directions: Read "Dan's Saturday" again. Write the sentence that goes with each picture.

1.	
2.	
3.	
4.	
5.	
6.	
7.	

Simple Present Affirmative: Quiz #1

Directions: Choose the correct form of the verb and write it in the blanks

eat or **eats**

1. I_____hamburgers.   5. It_____pet food.

2. You_____salads.   6. We_____dessert.

3. She_____sandwiches.   7. They_____fruit.

4. He_____meat.   8. Mike_____pizza.

watch or **watches**

9. My little brothers_____cartoons.

10. Dad_____the news.

11. Mom_____game shows.

12. You _____action movies.

13. My friend and I _____football and soccer games on TV.

14. My uncle_____police shows.

15. I_____animal shows.

16. My teacher_____the news, too.

take or **takes**

17. I_____a shower every morning.

18. Dad_____us to school.

19. My sister_____the bus to work.

20. My family_____vitamins every day.

21. We_____the metro to the museums.

22. You _____the bus to school.

23. They_____a taxi to the airport.

24. It_____a nap on the soft rug

Simple Present Affirmative: Quiz #1

work or works

25. My dad_____in Washington, DC.

26. My mom_____in Virginia.

27. My aunt and uncle_____in Maryland.

28. I _____in a restaurant.

29. They_____with a lawn service.

30. You_____after school.

31. We_____hard in school.

32. He_____at night.

carry or carries

33. Dad_____the heavy grocery bags.

34. I_____the light grocery bags.

35. Mom_____the baby.

36. My brother_____the boxes.

37. They_____the equipment to the field.

38. You _____your violin to music class.

39. We_____our lunch trays to the table.

have or has

40. I_____brown hair.

41. You_____blond hair.

42. She_____red hair.

43. He_____short hair.

44. We_____long hair.

45. They_____curly hair.

46. It_____green eyes.

47. I_____brown eyes.

48. My friend_____blue eyes.

49. She_____one brother.

50. I _____two sisters.

51. Mary_____two brothers.

Simple Present Affirmative: Quiz #2

Directions: Write the **"s"** form of the verbs by adding **"s,"** **"es**," or **"ies"** to the ends of the verbs.

* Remember the irregular verbs: **"do-does,"** **"go-goes,"** and **"have-has."**

1. brush -	11. hurry -
2. carry -	12. like -
3. clean -	13. make -
4. do -	14. play -
5. drink -	15. study -
6. eat -	16. take -
7. fix -	17. try -
8. give -	18. wash -
9. go -	19. watch -
10. have -	20. work -

4-13:

Simple Present Affirmative: Quiz #3

Directions: To begin, read the story "School Day."

School Day

Every morning I brush my teeth. I take a shower. I wash my hair. Then I go to the kitchen, and I eat breakfast. I drink orange juice. Then, I fix my lunch. After that, I go outside.

I hurry to school. I like school. I work hard at school. I study at school. I make good grades.

After school, I watch TV, and I play with my friends. I eat supper. Then I clean the kitchen. After that, I do my homework, and I go to bed.

Directions: Now that you have read the story "School Day," rewrite the story and change the pronoun from **"I"** to **"he."** Also, change **"my"** to **"his."**

Every morning **he** brush**es his** teeth. _____

_____

_____

_____

_____

_____

_____

_____

_____

Simple Present Affirmative: Quiz #4

Directions: Write 14 sentences in the Simple Present. Use the pronouns and nouns that are provided. Follow the example and write your own sentences.

1.	*You like pizza.*
2.	He
3.	I
4.	She
5.	We
6.	It
7.	They
8.	You
9.	My parents
10.	My friend
11.	Sandra
12.	Billy and I
13.	Billy and Joe
14.	Joe
15.	My friends

Chapter #5

Simple Present Tense - Negative

The Simple Present Negative

For the Simple Present Negative, make a sentence into a negative sentence by putting **"do not"** or **"does not"** before the verb.

* Notice that "**he**," "**she**," and "**it**" use the verb **"does."**

Examples:

Subject + *do not / does not* + Verb

I	do	not	talk in class.
You	do	not	talk in class.
He	**does**	not	talk in class.
She	**does**	not	talk in class.
It	**does**	not	talk in class.
We	do	not	talk in class.
You	do	not	talk in class.
They	do	not	talk in class.

* Also notice that the contractions **"don't"** and **"doesn't"** are commonly used.

* **"Do not"** = **"don't"** and **"does not"** = **"doesn't."**

Examples:

Subject + *don't / doesn't* + Verb

I	don't	talk in class.
You	don't	talk in class.
He	doesn't	talk in class.
She	doesn't	talk in class.
It	doesn't	talk in class.
We	don't	talk in class.
You	don't	talk in class.
They	don't	talk in class.

Simple Present Negative: "Don't"

* Use **"don't"** with **"I," "you," "we,"** and **"they."**

Directions: Make the following sentences negative by adding **"don't."** Rewrite the whole sentence and add **"don't"** to make it negative.

Subject + Verb	**Subject + don't + Verb**
Example: I talk in class.	*I **don't** talk in class.*

1. I make noise in class. _____

2. I like coffee. _____

3. You like coffee. _____

4. We like coffee. _____

5. They like coffee. _____

6. I speak English. _____

7. We speak French. _____

8. They speak Spanish. _____

9. You speak Portuguese. _____

10. They listen in class. _____

11. We know where to go. _____

12. They know the city very well. _____

13. I want to go. _____

14. They work in the same place. _____

15. I have enough money. _____

16. You have to work on Saturday. _____

17. We live close to the school. _____

18. They take music lessons. _____

19. I like the cold weather. _____

20. I play tennis. _____

21. You play hockey. _____

Directions: Choose a partner. One of you reads the affirmative sentence, (You play hockey), and one of you reads the negative sentence, (You **don't** play hockey).

Simple Present Negative: "Doesn't"

* There is no **"s"** on a verb when it is used with **"doesn't."**

Directions: Make the following sentences negative by adding **"doesn't."** Rewrite the whole sentence and add **"doesn't"** to make it negative.

Subject + Verb	**Subject + doesn't + Verb**
Example: He talks in class.	He *doesn't* talk in class. _____
1. He talks in the library.	_____
2. It barks at the mailman.	_____
3. He rides his bike to school.	_____
4. She drives a car to work.	_____
5. It runs after the mailman.	_____
6. She comes late to class.	_____
7. She speaks French.	_____
8. He speaks Spanish.	_____
9. She works at night.	_____
10. He works in construction.	_____
11. He drives a white truck.	_____
12. It digs holes in the yard.	_____
13. It digs up the flowers.	_____
14. He lives in Florida.	_____
15. It lives in that tree.	_____
16. He plays on that team.	_____

Directions: Choose a partner. One of you reads the affirmative sentence (He lives in Florida), and one of you reads the negative sentence (He doesn't live in Florida).

Simple Present Negative: "Don't" / "Doesn't"

* Remember that **"doesn't"** is used with "he," she," and "it." And remember that **"don't"** is used with "I," "you," "we," and "they."

Directions: Choose **"don't"** or **"doesn't"** to change the following sentences into the negative.

Subject + Verb	Subject + **don't / doesn't** + Verb
Example #1: He plays the guitar.	*He **doesn't** play the guitar*
Example #2: I play the piano.	*I **don't** play the piano.*

1. She plays the violin. _____

2. They play the drums. _____

3. We play in the band. _____

4. You play the trumpet. _____

5. It likes to play in the water. _____

6. She knows his name. _____

7. He knows where his wallet is. _____

8.   I know where I put my keys. _____

9.   You know what's wrong with it. _____

10. They know where their dog is. _____

11. We know where he is. _____

12. John knows the answer. _____

13. I have enough room for it. _____

Simple Present Negative: "Don't" / "Doesn't"

* Remember that **"doesn't"** is used with "he," she," and "it." And remember that **"don't"** is used with "I," "you," "we," and "they."

Directions: Choose **"don't"** or **"doesn't"** to change the following sentences into the negative.

Subject + Verb	Subject + **don't / doesn't** + Verb
14. They live here.	_____
15. I live in a big apartment.	_____
16. I have enough money.	_____
17. You have enough time.	_____
18. They have two cars.	_____
19. I like scary movies.	_____
20. She likes this food.	_____
21. They want to eat here.	_____
22. I want a hamburger.	_____
23. She wants to go.	_____
24. My dog likes to sit still.	_____
25. The children like their sitter.	_____
26. Frank likes his new job.	_____
27. Tom works on weekends.	_____
28. I have her phone number.	_____

Directions: Choose a partner. One of you reads the affirmative sentence (I have her phone number), and one of you reads the <u>negative</u> sentence (I <u>don't</u> have her phone number).

5-5:

Write Your Own Sentences: "Don't" / "Doesn't"

Directions: Write **4** sentences with **"don't"** and **4** sentences with **"doesn't."**

Don't
Example: *I **don't** have your book.*
1.
2.
3.
4.

Doesn't
Example: *She **doesn't** like broccoli.*
1.
2.
3.
4.

Directions: Choose a partner and read your sentences to each other.

Mrs. Garcia Is Angry

Directions: Read the story and answer the questions on the next page.

Mrs. Garcia has four children, and she is angry with all of them! She is angry with the twins because they don't pick up their toys, they don't eat their vegetables, and they don't go to bed on time. All they do is play. Mrs. Garcia is angry with her 15-year-old daughter, Sonya, because she doesn't wash the dishes, she doesn't clean up her room, and she doesn't baby-sit the twins. All she does is talk on the phone. Mrs. Garcia is angry with her 17-year-old son, Robert, because he doesn't take out the trash, he doesn't mow the lawn, and he doesn't do his homework. All he does is play basketball. Mrs. Garcia is disappointed and angry with her children.

Mrs. Garcia Is Angry

Directions: Answer the questions about the story in complete sentences.

Example:

1. Why is Mrs. Garcia angry with Sonya?

Mrs. Garcia is angry with Sonya because she doesn't wash the dishes.

Mrs. Garcia is angry with Sonya because she doesn't clean up her room.

Mrs. Garcia is angry with Sonya because she doesn't baby-sit the twins.

2. Why is Mrs. Garcia angry with the twins?

_____

_____

_____

3. Why is Mrs. Garcia angry with Robert?

_____

_____

_____

Mrs. Garcia Is Angry -
Writing Your Own Ideas

4. Why **might** Mrs. Garcia be angry with her husband? (You **make this up.**)

_____

_____

5. Why is your mother or father angry with **you**? (Think about this and write about something that is true in your life or make up something.)

_____

_____

6. Why is your brother or sister angry with **you**? (Think about this and write about something that is true or make up something.)

_____

_____

Directions: Choose a partner and read answers 4, 5, and 6 to each other.

Drama Activity: Why Is Everyone Angry?

Directions: Choose a partner. One of you is **"A"** and the other is **"B."**
Practice conversations #1, #2, #3, and #4.

* Try to include some **feelings and gestures** when you practice.

Conversation #1

A: Why is Joe's mother angry with him?

B: Joe's mother is angry with him because of these reasons.
    He doesn't clean his room.
    He doesn't do his homework.
    He doesn't take out the trash, and he doesn't help with the dishes!

A: Oh, that's why!

Conversation #2

B: Why is Mary's mother angry with her?

A: Mary's mother is angry with her because of these reasons.
    She doesn't stop talking on the phone.
    She doesn't pick up her clothes.
    She doesn't take care of the baby, and she doesn't feed the cat!

B: Oh, that's interesting!

Drama Activity: Why Is Everyone Angry?

Conversation #3

A: Why is Bob angry with me?

B: Bob is angry with you because of these reasons.
You don't sit with him on the bus.
You don't talk to him in the cafeteria.
You don't play basketball with him after school, and you don't share your snacks with him!

A: Thanks for telling me!

Conversation #4

B: Why is Annabell angry with me?

A: Annabell is angry with you because of these reasons.
You don't walk to school with her.
You don't sit with her at lunch.
You don't ride your bike with her, and you don't share your things with her!

B: So that's why she's angry with me!

Directions: The teacher will call on different pairs of students to perform one of the conversations.

Making Up Your Own Dialogue:
Why is Everyone Angry?

Conversation #5

Directions: Can you and your partner make up a conversation? Think about people in your life: friends, parents, children, spouse, neighbors, and relatives. Think about what makes them angry. You and your partner should discuss what makes them angry. Now you have a lot of ideas, and you are ready to write Conversation #5.

Conversation #5

A: Why is _____ angry with_____?

B: _____is angry with_____ for these reasons.

1. _____

   _____

2. _____

   _____

3. _____

   _____

A: Oh, that's why!

Directions: Go around the class and share your conversation with different people. You and your partner read your conversation. Then listen to another pair's conversation. Your teacher will ask for volunteers to share their Conversation #5 in front of the class.

Story and Student Writing: Totty Is a Bad Pet

Directions: Read the story.

Totty Is a Bad Pet

I love my little puppy, Totty, but sometimes Totty is a bad pet! Totty doesn't come when I call him, and he runs the other way! Totty doesn't like to take a bath, so he hides under the bed. Totty doesn't treat the cat right, so Totty chases the cat. Totty doesn't eat his own food, but he likes to beg for my food! Totty doesn't dig outside, but he likes to dig into my trash. Sometimes my little dog is bad, but I love my naughty little Totty!

Directions: Now that you have read a story about Totty, you can write a story. Think about a pet that you have or used to have. Write a short story about your pet being bad. An illustration would be good, too.

Class mixer: Go around the room and share your story with someone. Listen to his or her story, too. Keep doing this until the teacher tells you to stop.

The teacher will call on a few students to read their stories in front of the class.

Contrast with "Doesn't" - #1

Directions: Rewrite sentences #1 to 6 by following the first two examples.

Example #1: She doesn't eat candy. (fruit)
She doesn't eat candy. She eats fruit.

Example #2: He doesn't play basketball. (football)
He doesn't play basketball. He plays football.

1. Mr. Smith doesn't look old. (young)

2. Jane doesn't go to high school. (college)

3. My father doesn't work in Virginia. (Maryland)

4. Mother doesn't feel bad. (great)

5. My brother doesn't take piano lessons. (guitar lessons)

6. My sister doesn't like pears. (oranges)

Contrast with "Doesn't" - #1

7.   My friend **doesn't speak** Swahili. (Urdu)
     *My friend doesn't speak Swahili. My friend **speaks** Urdu.*

8.   My neighbor **doesn't like** rock music. (classical music)

9.   My grandmother **doesn't read** love stories. (historical novels)

Directions: Write 4 examples of your own.

     Example: He **doesn't like** ping pong. He **likes** tennis.

10.   _____

11.   _____

12.   _____

13.   _____

Contrast with "Doesn't" - #2

Directions: Rewrite sentences #1 to #5 by following the examples below.

Example #1: She **eats** cake. (pie)
*She eats cake. She **doesn't eat** pie.*

Example #2: She **eats** donuts. (cupcakes)
*She eats donuts. She **doesn't eat** cupcakes.*

1. He **eats** grapes. (strawberries)

2. My father **drinks** coffee. (tea)

3. It **wants** to run. (sit)

4. Wendy **speaks** French. (Amharic)

5. My brother **likes** hockey. (skateboarding)

Contrast with "Doesn't" - #2

6. My uncle **plays** cards. (chess)

7. My aunt **likes** to cook. (sew)

8. My sister **wants** to buy a sweater. (coat)

9. My mother **wants** to go to Florida. (New York)

Directions: Write 4 examples of your own sentences.

   Example: She **likes** to sing. She **doesn't like** to dance.

10. _____

11. _____

12. _____

13. _____

Contrast with "Don't" - #1

Directions: Rewrite the sentences by following this example.

> Example: I **don't eat** chips. (pretzels)
> *I don't eat chips. I **eat** pretzels.*

1. I **don't drink** soda. (juice)

2. We **don't want** to go to the movies. (dance)

3. They **don't live** in Austin. (San Antonio)

4. You **don't like** hot weather. (cold weather)

5. I **don't feel** bad. (good)

6. We **don't go** to Houston High School. (Hunter High School)

7. They **don't like** fast food. (healthy food)

8. You **don't know** my cell phone number. (home phone number)

9. I **don't like** to run. (walk)

10. We **don't paint** landscapes. (portraits)

Contrast with "Don't" - #2

Directions: Rewrite the sentences by following the example.

Example: I **eat** green beans. (broccoli)
*I eat green beans. I **don't eat** broccoli.*

1. I **eat** hamburgers. (hot dogs)

2. You **eat** sandwiches. (pizza)

3. We **play** baseball. (basketball)

4. They **fix** computers. (televisions)

5. They **play** football. (rugby)

6. We **like** volleyball. (tennis)

7. You **speak** Spanish. (French)

8. I **drink** tea. (coffee)

9. I **live** in the country. (city)

10. They **work** at Carson's Cars. (Tom's Trucks)

"Don't" / "Doesn't" Review: Lazy Larry

Directions: Read the story "Lazy Larry."

Lazy Larry

Hi. My name is Larry. I get so mad because everyone says I'm lazy. They say I'm lazy because I don't like to throw out the trash. I don't like to take my turn washing dishes. I don't like to help Mom cut the vegetables when she is cooking. I don't like to clean my room. I don't like to help clean up the house on Saturdays when everybody is cleaning it, and I don't like to baby-sit my little brother.

I'm not lazy! There are a lot of things I like to do. I like to play video games. I like to play basketball with my friends after school. I like to listen to music. I like to lie down and watch TV, and I like to be with my friends. People just don't understand me! I am not lazy! Don't you agree?

Directions: Now that you have read the story, answer the questions on the following two pages.

"Lazy Larry" Questions

1. Name 6 reasons why people say Larry is lazy.

_____

_____

_____

_____

_____

_____

2. Why does Larry say he is **not** lazy?

_____

_____

_____

_____

_____

3. Write 4 things you do to help at home.

_____

_____

_____

_____

4. Name 2 things you do but **don't like to do.**

_____

_____

_____

_____

"Lazy Larry" Questions

5. Do you think Larry is lazy or not lazy? Explain why you think that.

_____

_____

_____

_____

_____

_____

6. Do you know a lazy person? Why do you think this person is lazy?

_____

_____

_____

_____

_____

_____

Directions: Choose a partner and read your answers to question #6 to each other.

"Do Not" / "Does Not": Quiz #1

Directions: Choose **"do not"** or **"does not"** and fill in the blank with the correct choice.

1. I _____ have enough money to buy it.

2. You _____ have to work tomorrow.

3. He _____ live in my building.

4. She _____ go to school with me.

5. It _____ look like it is going to rain.

6. We _____ want to go.

7. They _____ have any relatives that live here.

8. Frank and Tom _____ work in the same store.

9. My father _____ work on the weekends.

10. Mother _____ like to skate.

11. My friend _____ want to go to that restaurant.

12. My friends _____ live close to me.

13. My dog _____ obey me.

14. James and I _____ get out of work at the same time.

15. I _____ know how to do this.

Directions: Write 3 sentences with **"do not."**

1. _____

2. _____

3. _____

Directions: Write 3 sentences with **"does not."**

1. _____

2. _____

3. _____

"Don't" / "Doesn't": Quiz #2

Directions: Write your own examples of sentence pairs that use **"don't"** and **"doesn't."** Write 2 examples for each. Base your sentences on the examples.

1. She **doesn't** eat candy. She eats fruit.

_____

_____

2. She eats cake. She **doesn't** eat pie.

_____

_____

3. I **don't** eat chips. I eat pretzels.

_____

_____

4. I eat green beans. I **don't** eat broccoli.

_____

_____

Story Quiz: Quiz #3

Directions: Read the story.

Nobody Likes Us

Everybody is irritated and angry with Nan and the twins. Nan and the twins feel like nobody likes them!

Mother is angry with Nan because Nan doesn't speak respectfully to her. Father is angry with Nan because she doesn't help around the house. The teacher is angry with Nan because she doesn't stop talking in class. Nan's friends are angry with her because she borrows things and doesn't return them. Nan is feeling very sad because everyone is angry with her.

The twins are sad, too. Father is angry with them because they don't do their homework. They just play video games. Mother is angry with them because they don't do their chores. Their teacher is angry with them because they don't listen in class. Their soccer team is angry with them because they don't get to practice on time. They are always late. Poor children, everyone is angry with them! They feel that nobody likes them!

Directions: Answer these questions about "Nobody Likes Us" in complete sentences.

1. Why is mother angry with Nan?

2. Why are Nan's friends angry with her?

3. Why is the soccer team angry with the twins?

Nobody Likes Us – Application:
What about You?

Directions: Think about the following questions and answer them in complete sentences.

1. Why is your mother angry with you?

2. Why is your teacher angry with you?

3. Why are your friends angry with you?

4. Who are you angry with? Why?

What Kind of Food Do You Like?

Group #1: Fruit

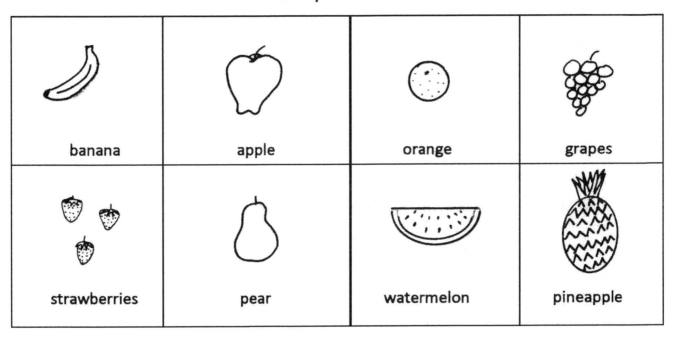

banana	apple	orange	grapes
strawberries	pear	watermelon	pineapple

Group #2: Vegetables

carrots	potatoes	peas	lettuce	pepper
squash	corn	cabbage	green beans	tomatoes

What Kind of Food Do You Like?

Group #3: Meat

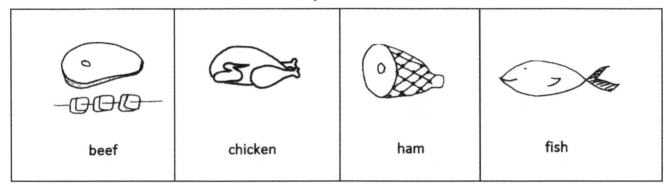

| beef | chicken | ham | fish |

Group #4: Dairy

| milk | cheese | butter | eggs |

Group #5: Bread

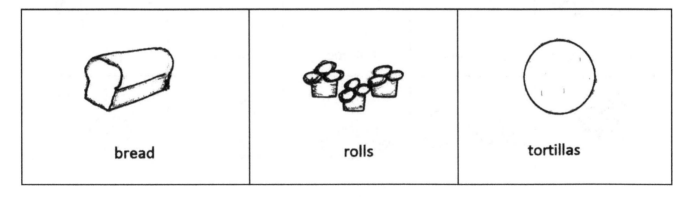

| bread | rolls | tortillas |

What Kind of Food Do You Like?

Group #6: Drinks

coffee	iced tea	juice	water
milk	soft drink	hot chocolate	lemonade

Group #7: Prepared Food

hamburger	french fries	hot dog	pizza	tacos
spaghetti	salad	soup	sandwich	rice

What Kind of Food Do You Like?

Group #8: Desserts / Sweets

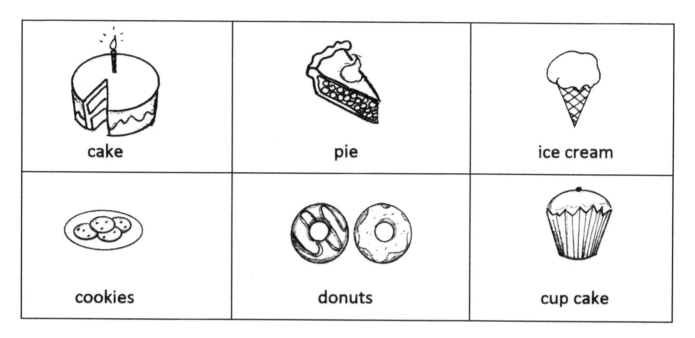

Group #9: Snacks

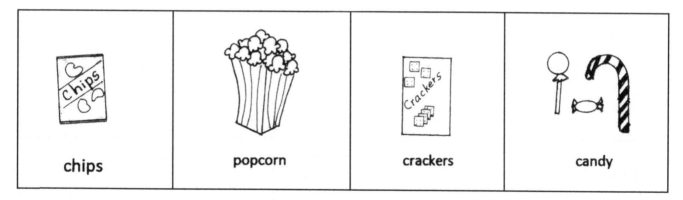

Directions: Think about all the food that you've reviewed. On the next page, write one food from each group that you **like** and one that you **don't like**. Examples:

Food Groups	I like _____.	I don't like _____.
Example: Prepared Food	I **like** hamburgers.	I **don't like** hot dogs.
Example: Fruit	I **like** peaches.	I **don't like** oranges.

Foods That I Like and Foods That I Don't Like

Food Groups	I like _____.	I don't like _____.
Example: Fruit	I **like** apples.	I **don't like** bananas.
Fruit		
Vegetables		
Meat		
Dairy		
Bread		
Drinks		
Prepared Food		
Desserts/Sweets		
Snacks		

Food Survey

Go around the room and ask people the question below. Keep a tally of how many people say "yes" and how many people say "no."

"Do you like_____?"

(one of the foods or drinks that we learned about)

Yes_____

No_____

Reporting on Your Food Survey

The teacher will call on the students to go before the class to report on their surveys. An example of your report should look like this:

> **I asked <u>12</u> students this question:**
> **"Do you like <u>hamburgers</u>?"**
> **<u>7</u> students said "yes."**
> **<u>5</u> students said "no."**

Fill in your information and report:

> **I asked _____ students this question:**
> **"Do you like_____?"**
> **_____said "yes."**
> **_____said "no."**

Food Quiz

1. Name 2 fruits: _____, _____

2. Name 2 vegetables: _____, _____

3. Name 2 meats: _____, _____

4. Name 2 drinks: _____, _____

5. Name 1 dairy product: _____

6. Name 1 dessert: _____

7. Name 1 snack: _____ _____

8. Name 4 prepared foods: _____, _____

_____, _____

Word Box: Spelling Help

Apple	Cookies	Milk	Rolls
Banana	Donuts	Onions	Salad
Beef	Fish	Orange	Sandwich
Bread	Grapes	Pear	Soup
Butter	Green beans	Peas	Squash
Cabbage	Hamburger	Pie	Strawberries
Carrot	Hot dog	Pineapple	Tacos
Cheese	Ice cream	Pizza	Tea
Chicken	Juice	Popcorn	Tortillas
Chips	Lemonade	Potato	Water
Coffee	Lettuce	Rice	Watermelon

Chapter #6

Simple Present Tense - Questions

Simple Present Questions
Overview

Simple Present Questions are formed by putting **"do"** or **"does"** before the subject.

Do / Does + Subject + Verb

Do I like to play?

Do you like to play?

* Does he like to play?

* Does she like to play?

* Does it like to play?

Do we like to play?

Do you like to play?

Do they like to play?

* Do not put **"s"** on the verb. The **"s"** is already on "does."

These are called **"yes"** / **"no"** questions because they can be answered with a **"yes"** / **"no"** short answer.

Simple Present Questions
Overview of "Yes" / "No" Short Answers

* **Short Answers:** These are called **"yes"** / **"no"** questions because they can be answered with a **"yes"** or **"no"** short answer.

Question	"Yes" Short Answer	"No" Short Answer	"No" Short Answer (abbreviations)
Do they like pizza?	Yes, they do.	No, they do not.	No, they don't.
Does he like pizza?	Yes, he does.	No, he does not.	No, he doesn't.
Does she like pizza?	Yes, she does.	No, she does not.	No, she doesn't.
Does it like pizza?	Yes, it does.	No, it does not.	No, it doesn't.
Do I like pizza?	Yes, you do.	No, you do not.	No, you don't.
Do I like pizza? (I'm asking myself.)	Yes, I do.	No, I do not.	No, I don't.
Do we like pizza?	Yes, you do.	No, you do not.	No, you don't.
Do we like pizza? (We're asking ourselves.)	Yes, we do.	No, we do not.	No, we don't.
Do you like pizza?	Yes, I do.	No, I do not.	No, I don't.
Do you like pizza? (plural)	Yes, we do.	No, we do not.	No, we don't.

Simple Present Questions – "Do"
Practice Making Questions with "Do"

Directions: Change these sentences to questions by adding **"Do"** to the beginning of each sentence and by adding a question mark to the end of the sentence.

Examples: They live in New York.
                             Do they live in New York?

                             I know you.
                             Do *I know you?*

1. You go to Florida every summer.

2. You like country music.

3. They go to Maple High School.

4. They work in Virginia.

5. They work at Big Burger.

6. We have a test on Friday.

7. We get out of school in June.

Practice Making Questions with "Do"

8. Billy and I have to clean the yard.

9. Mr. and Mrs. Mack live there.

10. You want some coffee.

11. I have to do the laundry.

12. You work here.

13. You live here.

14. Mr. and Mrs. Garza like to sail.

15. They have a boat.

16. Jim and I work tomorrow night.

17. You watch the news on TV.

Directions: Choose a partner. You read the sentences, and your partner reads the questions. Then switch. Your partner reads the sentences, and you read the questions.

Simple Present Questions – "Does"
Practice Making Questions with "Does"

Directions: Change these sentences to questions by adding **"Does"** to the beginning of each sentence.

* Remember to remove the **"s"** from the verb when you are using **"does."**

Example #1:	He like<u>s</u> fried chicken.
	Does he like fried chicken?

Example #2:	He likes pepperoni pizza.
	Does he like pepperoni pizza?

1. He works after school.

2. He plays soccer.

3. She listens to rock and roll music.

4. She works every weekend.

5. She watches soap operas on TV.

6. It snows in January.

7. It rains in March.

Simple Present Questions – "Does"
Practice Making Questions with "Does"

8. It gets cold at night.

9. It chases the cat.

10. Mr. Kent coaches the football team.

11. He coaches the baseball team, too.

12. Anita sells cakes.

13. She sells pies, too.

14. The store opens at 8 o'clock.

15. It closes at 6 o'clock.

16. He plays soccer.

17. She plays tennis.

18. It runs fast.

Directions: Choose a partner. You read the sentences, and your partner reads the questions. Then switch. Your partner reads the sentences, and you read the questions.

Simple Present Questions – "Do" / "Does"

Directions: Form questions by adding **"Do"** or **"Does"** to the beginning of each sentence.

* Use **"Does"** for **"he,"** **"she,"** and **"it."** Use **"Do"** for "**I,**" **"you,"** **"we,"** and **"they."**

> Example #1:   You live in Los Angeles.
> ***Do** you live in Los Angeles?*

> Example #2:   He works in San Antonio.
> ***Does** he work in San Antonio?*

1. She lives on the second floor.

2. I need to bring the sandwiches.

3. We have math homework.

4. They ride the bus.

5. The bank opens at 9 o'clock.

6. Joe drinks coffee.

7. They know how to get here.

8. Helen plays the piano.

9. Ben likes video games.

Simple Present Questions – "Do" / "Does"

10. You want to sit here.

11. It snows in Michigan.

12. Mr. and Mrs. Green take golf lessons.

13. We have to finish it today.

14. I take this medicine every morning.

15. He feels sick.

16. It rains in the spring.

17. We need to call the manager.

18. They know what time they should be here.

19. You know what time it is.

Directions: You read the sentences, and your partner reads the questions. Then switch. Now your partner reads the sentences, and you read the questions.

Write Your Own Questions – "Does"

Directions: Use this chart to write 10 questions. Choose one word or phrase from each column to make a question.

Does	he she it	like	popcorn? cheese? donuts? pizza? pineapple juice? orange juice? milk? coffee? to play basketball? to play ping pong? to play soccer? to read graphic novels? to read detective stories? to read scary stories?

1. _____?

2. _____?

3. _____?

4. _____?

5. _____?

6. _____?

7. _____?

8. _____?

9. _____?

10. _____?

Write Your Own Questions – "Do"

Directions: Use this chart to write 10 questions. Choose one word or phrase from each column to make a question.

Do	you they we I	like	to watch comedies on TV? to watch action movies? to watch cartoons? to eat seafood? to eat dessert? to travel? to swim? to hike? to play cards? to play board games?

1. _____?

2. _____?

3. _____?

4. _____?

5. _____?

6. _____?

7. _____?

8. _____?

9. _____?

10. _____?

Directions: Choose a partner. Read your questions to each other.

Quizzing My Friend – "Yes, I Do" or "No, I Don't"

Directions: Choose a partner. First you ask the questions and your partner answers, then your partner asks the questions and you answer. Remember to answer **"Yes, I do"** or **"No, I don't."** Do not write the answer but just practice speaking.

Questions	"Yes, I do."	"No, I don't."
1. Do you live in _____?		
2. Do you speak_____?		
3. Do you ride the bus?		
4. Do you have a brother?		
5. Do you have a sister?		
6. Do you like to play _____?		
7. Do you like to eat_____?		
8. Do you like to drink_____?		
9. Do you like to watch _____on TV?		
10. Do you like to read_____?		
11. Do you like to go to the _____?		
12. _____?		

Directions: Find another partner and do the same thing. You are trying to learn how to ask questions with **"do"** and how to answer with a **"Yes"** or **"No"** short answer.

Practicing "Yes" / "No" Short Answers

Directions: Answer these questions with a "**yes**" or "**no**" short answer. Answer as truthfully as you can. Write the answers in the blanks.

"Yes, I do" or "No, I don't."

1. Do you have long hair? _____.
2. Do you have short hair? _____.
3. Do you have a brother? _____.
4. Do you have a sister? _____.
5. Do you have brown eyes? _____.
6. Do you have blue eyes? _____.

"Yes, we do" or "No, we don't."

7. Do you and your family live in the country? _____.
8. Do you and your family live in the city? _____.
9. Do you and your family like hot weather? _____.
10. Do you and your family like cold weather? _____.
11. Do you and your family live in Texas? _____.
12. Do you and your family like to go camping? _____.
13. Do you and your family like to go fishing? _____.

"Yes, they do" or "No, they don't."

14. Do your parents have a truck? _____.
15. Do your parents have a car? _____.
16. Do your neighbors have a motorcycle? _____.
17. Do your neighbors have children? _____.
18. Do your neighbors have a pet? _____.

Practicing "Yes" / "No" Short Answers

> "Yes, she does" or "No, she doesn't."

---

19. Does your mother wear glasses? _____.

20. Does your grandmother like to cook? _____.

21. Does your mother like to play basketball? _____.

22. Does your mother like hot tea? _____.

23. Does your mother have long hair? _____.

24. Does your grandmother have short hair? _____.

> "Yes, he does" or "No, he doesn't."

---

25. Does your father like to play cards? _____.

26. Does your father have blue eyes? _____.

27. Does your father play the guitar? _____.

28. Does your father like to play soccer? _____.

29. Does your father have a sister? _____.

30. Does your father have a brother? _____.

Directions: Choose a partner. Your partner asks you the questions, and you answer.
Then you ask the questions, and your partner answers.

* If you need help, look at Section 5-1 for a quick review of short answers. You and
your partner can also practice speaking with 5-1.

Betty

Betty has long red hair and big green eyes. She is tall and thin. Many people think that Betty is beautiful.

Betty is a nice person, too. Betty is friendly to everyone at the library where she works. She smiles at everyone that comes in. She tries to help everybody in any way that she can. She goes out of her way to help old people. She remembers what they like, and she tells them about all the new books that come in. People think Betty is beautiful inside and out.

Directions: After reading the story "Betty," answer the following questions with a **"yes"** or **"no"** short answer.

Example: Does Betty work in a library?   **Yes, she does**_____.

1. Does Betty have blue eyes?   _____.

2. Does Betty have green eyes?   _____.

3. Does Betty have short hair?   _____.

4. Does Betty have long hair?   _____.

5. Do people think that Betty is beautiful?   _____.

6. Does Betty try to be helpful?   _____.

7. Does Betty only help old people?   _____.

8. Do people think that Betty is ugly?   _____.

9. Do people think that Betty is beautiful inside and out? _____.

Directions: Choose a partner. One of you reads the questions, and the other reads the answers.

"Do" / "Does" Questions: Speaking Activity

Directions: Think of a male relative, such as your father, brother, or uncle. Fill out the information below in **Box #1** by using **Box #2** for a list of choices for filling in the blanks.

Box #1: Information for a Male Relative

1. My relative's name is _____.

2. He gets up at_____.

3. He likes to drink _____.

4. He likes to eat _____.

5. He likes to play _____.

6. He also likes to _____.

Box #2: Fill in the Blanks in Box #1 with the Answers Below

1.   **name** of your relative

2. The time your relative **gets up**: 4:00 4:30 5:00 5:30 6:00 6:30 7:00 7:30 8:00 8:30 9:00 9:30 10:00

3. What your relative likes to **drink**: milk coffee tea water orange juice milk shakes apple juice soft drinks

4. What your relative likes to **eat**: hamburgers hot dogs pizza spaghetti salad soup stir-fry rice tacos egg rolls sushi pupusas vegetables lentils sandwiches chicken fish ham beef steak

5. What your relative likes to **play:** tennis soccer basketball football baseball volleyball video games cards

6. Something your relative **also likes to do**: ride a bike go swimming go fishing dance listen to music watch TV go to the movies walk roller skate hike read

"Do" / "Does" Questions: Speaking Activity

Directions: Think of a female relative, such as your mother, sister, or aunt. Fill out the information below in **Box #1** by using **Box #2** for a list of choices for filling in the blanks.

Box #1: Information for a Female Relative

1. My relative's name is _____.

2. She gets up at_____.

3. She likes to drink _____.

4. She likes to eat _____.

5. She likes to play _____.

6. She also likes to _____.

Box #2: Fill in the Blanks in Box #1 with the Answers Below

1. ____ **name** of your relative ____

2. The time your relative **gets up**:   4:00   4:30   5:00   5:30   6:00   6:30   7:00   7:30   8:00   8:30   9:00   9:30   10:00

3. What your relative likes to **drink**: milk   coffee   tea   water   orange juice   milk shakes   apple juice   soft drinks

4. What your relative likes to **eat**: hamburgers   hot dogs   pizza   spaghetti   salad   soup   stir-fry   rice   tacos   egg rolls   sushi   pupusas   vegetables   lentils   sandwiches   chicken   fish   ham   beef steak

5. What your relative likes to **play**:   tennis   soccer   basketball   football   baseball   volleyball   video games   cards

6. Something your relative **also likes to do**: ride a bike   go swimming   go fishing   dance   listen to music   watch TV   go to the movies   walk   roller skate   read   hike

"Do" / "Does" Questions: Speaking Activity
Asking Questions about the Relative

Directions: Choose a partner. You are going **to guess the information** about your partner's relative. **Keep guessing** until you get the **right answer.**

Example:

YOU	PARTNER
Does he get up at 7:00?	No, he doesn't.
Does he get up at 7:30?	No, he doesn't.
Does he get up at 8:00?	Yes, he does.

YOU	PARTNER
1. What is your relative's name?	His / her name is_____.
2. Does he/she **get up** at_____?	"Yes, he/she does," or "No, he/she doesn't."
3. Does he/she like to **drink** _____?	"Yes, he/she does," or "No, he/she doesn't."
4. Does he/she like to **eat**_____?	"Yes, he/she does," or "No, he/she doesn't."
5. Does he/she like to **play**_____?	"Yes, he/she does," or "No, he/she doesn't."
6. Does he/she **also like to**_____?	"Yes, he/she does," or "No, he/she doesn't."

Notes on this activity:

*It is very important that you ask the **full question each time.**

*It is also very important that you give the **full short answer** each time:

> **"Yes, he does."**   or   **"No, he doesn't."**

*If you do this speaking exercise correctly, you are going to learn how to ask questions correctly and how to answer correctly. You are going to learn it because you are going to get a lot of practice.

"Wh" Questions - Overview

Directions: Read the following information on **"Wh"** questions.

* You practiced the **"Yes" / "No"** questions. There are other types of questions, too. There are information questions called **"Wh"** questions because they start with question words **"who," "where," "when," "why,"** and **"what."** These questions ask for more information besides a **"yes"** or a **"no."**

* **"Do"** and **"does"** are sometimes used with **"Wh"** questions. The same rules apply. Use **"do"** with **"I," "you," "we,"** and **"they."** Use **"does"** with **"he," "she,"** and **"it."** Put **"do"** or **"does"** before the subject.

Rule: Put **"do"** before the _subject_.
Example: _Where **do** you want me to meet you?_

Rule: Put **"does"** before the _subject_.
Example: _Where **does** she live?_

Example "Wh" questions:

"Wh"ere	do/does	Subject	Verb
1. Where	**do**	_I_	live?
2. Where	**do**	_you_	live?
3. Where	**does**	_she_	live?
4. Where	**does**	_he_	live?
5. Where	**does**	_it_	live?
6. Where	**do**	_we_	live?
7. Where	**do**	_you_	live?
8. Where	**do**	_they_	live?

"Wh" Questions #1
"Who," "What," "Where," "When," "Why" + "Do" / "Does"

Directions: Fill in the blanks with **"do"** or **"does."**

Example: What _____**do**_____ I want?

What + do / does

1. What _____ you want?

2. What _____ he want?

3. What _____ she want?

4. What _____ it want?

5. What _____ we want?

6. What _____ they want?

7. What time _____ the movie start?

8. What time _____ the bus get here?

9. What time _____ you leave for work?

10. What _____ you want to do?

11. What _____ you want to play?

12. What _____ he need?

13. What _____ she look like?

14. What _____ you need?

"Wh" Questions #2

Directions: Fill in the blanks with **"do"** or **"does."**

Where + do / does

Example: Where __does__ she live?

1. Where _____ your brother go to school?

2. Where _____ you live?

3. Where _____ she buy her clothes?

4. Where _____ we put our test papers?

5. Where _____ it hurt?

6. Where _____ I sit?

7. Where _____ they live?

When + do / does

Example: When ___does___ the bell ring?

1. When _____ you want me to pick you up?

2. When _____ he go to work?

3. When _____ she have her doctor's appointment?

4. When _____ the store open?

5. When _____ they leave for vacation?

"Wh" Questions #3

Directions: Fill in the blanks with **"do"** or **"does."**

Why + do / does

Example: Why ____do____ I always have to wash the dishes?

1. Why _____ she always get to go first?

2. Why _____ you stay up so late?

3. Why _____ he always sit by himself?

4. Why _____ we have homework every night?

5. Why _____ they complain so much?

6. Why _____ it snow so much in Minnesota?

Who + do / does

Example: Who ____does____ he like?

1. Who _____ she walk home with?

2. Who _____ you sit with at lunch?

3. Who _____ they play next Saturday?

4. Who _____ we report this to?

Directions: Choose a partner. Take turns reading the questions to each other.

Questions: Quiz #1

Directions: Change these sentences to questions by adding **"Do"** or **"Does."**

Example #1: They work at Andy's Auto Shop.
Do *they work at Andy's Auto Shop?*

Example #2: She lives in New York.
Does *she live in New York?*

1. We have homework.

2. He plays the drums.

3. You live in Maryland.

4. It snows in Alaska.

5. The neighbors have a dog.

6. Joe drives a big blue truck.

7. Sue and Mary work in the same place.

8. I need to take this medicine twice a day.

Questions: Quiz #2

Directions: Fill in the blanks with **"do"** or **does."**

do / does

Example: What _____**do**_____ you want?

1. What _____ it like to eat?

2. Where _____ we park the car?

3. Where _____ she live?

4. Why _____ he walk instead of drive?

5. Why _____ we have to go?

6. When _____ they open the store?

7. When _____ the movie start?

8. Who _____ she like?

9. Who _____ this sweater belong to?

10. What _____ he need?

11. Where _____ you want to go?

12. When _____ the bell ring?

13. Who _____ she sit with at lunch?

14. What _____ you need?

15. Where _____ he work?

16. When _____ he go into work?

17. Who_____ I call to report this?

Questions - Short Answers: Quiz #3

Directions: Read the story.

Jack, Tom, and Billy

Jack, Tom, and Billy are cousins. Jack is short and muscular. He has short black hair and green eyes. Tom is tall and thin. He has blond hair and blue eyes. Billy has curly brown hair and brown eyes. These three cousins are always together.

People think they look alike! Maybe it is because they act the same, they talk the same, and they like the same things. They like cars. They are always working on cars and talking about cars. I guess they are the same in some ways, but not in their looks!

Directions: Answer the questions with a **"yes"** or **"no"** short answer.

Example: Does Jack have red hair? _____No, he doesn't_____.

1. Does Tom have blond hair? _____.

2. Does Billy have blue eyes? _____.

3. Does Tom have blue eyes? _____.

4. Does Jack have green eyes? _____.

5. Do the three cousins act the same? _____.

6. Do the three cousins like the same things?_____.

7. Do the three cousins like bikes? _____.

8. Do the cousins like cars? _____.

Questions: Quiz #4

Directions: Write 5 questions with **"do."**

Example #1: ***Do*** *you want to play football?*

Example #2: *What **do** you want?*

1. _____.

2. _____.

3. _____.

4. _____.

5. _____.

Directions: Write 5 questions with **"does."**

Example #1: ***Does*** *he like pizza?*

Example #2: *Where **does** she live?*

1. _____.

2. _____.

3. _____.

4. _____.

5. _____.

Books may be ordered through Amazon:

www.amazon.com

About Chris Balli

* Master's in Education in Curriculum and Instruction with a concentration in TESOL, University of Maryland, College Park

* 25 years of experience as an ESOL teacher in the public schools of Maryland and Connecticut

* 21 years of experience with students who had gaps in their educations or who were illiterate

* 25 years of writing curriculum to meet the needs of these students

Coming Soon!

English Language Learning with Super Support:
A WORKBOOK FOR ESL / ESOL / EFL / ELL STUDENTS
*Beginners – **Book 3***

English Language Learning with Super Support:
A WORKBOOK FOR ESL / ESOL / EFL / ELL Students
*Beginners – **Book 4***

Books may be ordered through Amazon at

www.amazon.com

Questions? Comments? Contact the author at sscballi@gmail.com

Made in the USA
Coppell, TX
30 November 2020